Huntsville Botanical Garden

Anita Hoodless

*Who **loves** a garden*
Finds within his soul
Life's whole...

—*Louise Seymore Jones*

Huntsville's Botanical Garden is a place where the seeds of dreams and ideas take root and grow into a magnificent and beautiful reality. It's a place where willing hands and hearts combine to shape the earth and young minds. It's a place where our community celebrates growth, renewal, love, and life.

The idea of the Garden sprang from the fertile minds of fourteen determined people in 1979; for almost ten years, they labored tirelessly through red clay, red tape, sun, and rain, until the Huntsville Botanical Garden opened to the public on May 21, 1988. Today, the Garden is one of the Tennessee Valley's premier attractions. In the midst of a high-tech city that's better known for helping to put a man on the moon, the Garden offers a changing landscape with every season, delighting more than 250,000 visitors annually.

You might begin your tour at the site of a magnificent one-hundred-year-old dogwood, saved from demolition during highway construction in 1995—revealing the dedication that Huntsville Botanical Garden exhibits in all its efforts at beautification, education, and preservation. The tree is just to the east of the southern terminus of the Dogwood Trail, a path that meanders through an upland forest, sprinkled throughout with numerous flowering dogwood trees. The trail serves as the western border of the Central Corridor Gardens and is a popular path that the community enjoys.

Lead your children in a search for toads, butterflies, and ladybugs among the beautiful plants and flowers. Unlike some of the more staid and formal gardens in the South, the Huntsville Botanical Garden welcomes children; they come with their families and they come in school groups, in numbers reaching over 12,000 every year.

The nation's largest seasonal butterfly house and nature center are here. Take your time, and soon even the shyest of creatures will flutter by for your enjoyment. There are more than a dozen species of North American butterflies in the house! The two-acre Children's Garden features a great lawn surrounded by eight specialty gardens. The Space, Maze, and Dinosaur Gardens are highlights, as are the many water features designed to delight the young visitors.

During the summer, there are demonstration vegetable gardens and public programs to help even the most inexperienced have a successful home garden. Visitors can learn about composting and earthworms, and are even given helpful instruction from the experts on reducing joint and muscle soreness after a day of enthusiastic gardening!

Flower lovers find spring one of the best times to visit, with thousands of tulips, daffodils, pansies, wildflowers, and azaleas constantly in bloom and looking good, in part, due to the efforts of over 1500 dedicated volunteers. Throughout the year, there are daylily, fern, and herb festivals, tours of local gardens, music, and entertainment.

The five-acre Central Corridor Gardens are ablaze with color from spring to fall. The Perennial Garden features a broad selection especially suited to the Tennessee Valley. As the largest component of the Central Corridor Gardens, this Garden is designed with sweeps of flower beds lining the grass allee and a river of emerald green flowing through the beds from the Entry Court to the Aquatic Garden in the distance—a wide semi-circle filled with water lilies, water lotus, and other tropical water plants.

The Bulb and Annual Garden displays a wide range of tender plants and bulbs, and is one of the major color attractions of the garden. The swirling, curving beds of the Ribbon Garden contain flowering shrubs that provide attractive displays in all seasons.

On top of all this, if you're visiting North Alabama between Thanksgiving and New Year's Eve, there's an event you won't want to miss: Huntsville Botanical Garden's Galaxy of Lights. This magnificent 1.5 mile drive-through holiday light extravaganza has garnered national attention and named to the Southeastern Tourism Society's Top Twenty Events several consecutive years. Animated light displays fill the Garden's 112-acre site. Enjoy traditional holiday scenes such as skaters, quaint villages, candy canes, and a Santa soaring overhead on a magnificent sleigh—a grand finale to another exciting year at the Garden.

Now it's your turn to visit our wonderful Garden—where beauty reigns, and life is constantly restored, and something is always growing on!

Special thanks to the Garden Guild for their efforts in making the Huntsville Sketchbook a success.

Huntsville Botanical Garden
Huntsville, Alabama 35805
(256) 830-4447
(256) 830-5314 fax
www.hsvbg.org

Huntsville Sketchbook

Foreword by Homer Hickam
Story by Jacquelyn Procter Gray
Paintings by Local Artists
Huntsville Botanical Garden, Benefactor

Indigo Custom Publishing

Publisher	Henry S. Beers
Associate Publisher	Richard J. Hutto
Executive Vice President	Robert G. Aldrich
Operations Manager	Gary G. Pulliam
Editor-in-Chief	Joni Woolf
Art Director/Designer	Julianne Gleaton
Designer	Daniel Emerson
Director of Marketing and Public Relations	Mary D. Robinson
Project Coordinator	Bill Koons

© 2006 by Indigo Custom Publishing

Cover art by: Barclay Burns

Printed in China.

Library of Congress Control Number: 2006931646

ISBN: (10 Digit) 0-9776711-5-1
(13 Digit) 978-0-9776711-5-1

Indigo custom books are available at quantity discounts with bulk purchase for educational, business, or sales promotional use. For information, please write to: Indigo Custom Publishing, SunTrust Bank Building, 435 Second Street, Suite 320, Macon, GA 31201 or call 866-311-9578.

Huntsville Sketchbook

Ed Starnes

Table of Contents

The Artists

First row (left to right): Dee Burt Holmes, Katrina Weber, Teresia Reid, Ann Caudle, Linda Morton, Peggy Montano,
Dorothy Montgomery, Linda Steed, Patricia Hrivnak, Denise Schiber

Second row: Carole Forêt, Staten Tate, Carla Swinney, Sherman Barnes, Susan Clanton, M.J. (Martha) Montgomery,
Heike Covell, Linda Ruhl, Denise Raby, Terri Shows, Anita Hoodless, Judith Fields, Rachel C. Heeschen, Malinda McCleary

Third row: Ed Starnes, Billy Herrin, Robert Sallee, David Kennamer, Jerry Brown, S. Renee Prasil, Lesile Lockhart, Ben L. Patton,
Helen J. Vaughn, Fred B. Simpson, Lee Harless

Dee Burt Holmes

Foreword by Homer Hickam

Huntsville is the kind of place that welcomes everyone. I first came here in 1969, after a tour of duty with the infantry in Vietnam. The optimism of Huntsville nurtured me then, as it does now. There is a vibrant energy to this place, a sense that the past was glorious but nothing compared to the future. I love the cosmopolitan people of this great city, and the rich, green valley it snuggles within, and the ancient mountains that rise above it. I love the Tennessee River that sweeps past Huntsville with such infinite and steady purpose, suggesting the timelessness of the city itself. Huntsville's citizens look forward, proper for a people on their way to the stars, but they also don't forget their past. The Space and Rocket Center, marked by its towering Saturn V rocket, is an active place, but so also is Constitution Village, where the pioneers of the city are celebrated. Churches, busy, well-attended, and active, abound everywhere. The arts are alive and well. There's a wonderful symphony, several dynamic theater groups, a Museum of Art, a first-class and well-used library system, all easily accessible. The Von Braun Center complex brings us the world of entertainment. The sports community is energetic. We Huntsvillians are hikers, bicyclers, runners, golfers, tennis players, or whatever else strikes us as healthy and fun.

But we also work. Oh, yes. Huntsville is a place for work. Work led me to Redstone Arsenal and thence to NASA where I helped engineer the Spacelab, Space Station, and Hubble Space Telescope programs. Every day, I woke up and thought to myself, "Oh, boy, I get to go to work!" That thought is pure Huntsvillian, for here industry is always welcome. Established companies and new-start entrepreneurs find a well-educated people, eager to roll up their sleeves and go to work. Great universities make their home here, guaranteeing a steady flow of bright, young people into Huntsville's business and high-tech communities. Listen to our industrial song. The chorus is strong, energetic, and rising.

When another career came to me, that of writing, I was more successful than I could imagine. One day, I realized I could live anywhere. After giving it some thought, my decision was to stay put. Huntsville is my home and a man who doesn't want to be home is a sad creature, isn't he? I observe with satisfaction the seasons of my town, the quiet, brittle winters, the glorious, bursting springs, the vast, green summers, and the magnificent, burnished autumns. I stroll through the Botanical Garden or the grounds of Dr. Burritt's historical estate. I peek at the stars at the observatory named after our own Dr. Wernher von Braun, who took our nation to the moon. I wander the trails of Monte Sano State Park. I hear the laughter of the children at Space Camp, or the Huntsville Depot, or Early Works. If there is a better place than Huntsville to live and nurture a family, I haven't found it and I've been around the world more than once.

We who live here tend to keep our fair city a secret, as if it were a hidden treasure. In some ways, it is. But, inevitably, more folks will discover it, and come here to work or to play. No matter what may bring them here, I know they will fall in love with Huntsville, just as I did so long ago. Welcome, I say. You have discovered a place where dreams and reality are often the same. Come and stay a while. It won't surprise me if you decide to stay forever.

The Aquatic Pavillion over the Water Lily Pool is a beloved part of the Huntsville Botanical Garden.

John Hunt's Spring

"You will expect something of this flourishing town," wrote Anne Newport Royall to a friend in 1818. She bragged that the workmanship of the buildings was the best she had ever seen. Not bad for a fledgling community. Even before statehood, the residents of Huntsville were preparing a model town—a place they could be proud of.

Tennessee native John Hunt stayed at the Criner home near the present-day community of New Market. The year was 1805, and the settler, thought by some to be a veteran of the American Revolution, learned of an area fifteen miles south, where the water was fresh, the hunting was good, and the soil was rich. The Indians referred to it simply as the Big Spring. Hunt found the information was true indeed, but he had more to do than clear the land and build a cabin. He would not tolerate the infestation of rattlesnakes! In time he won the battle, brought his family to Alabama, and named his stake Hunt's Spring.

On July 23, 1805, the Chickasaw Indians ceded their property to the United States government and in 1806, the Cherokees ceded their property as well. Neighboring states and territories were gripped with Alabama Fever. Settlers poured in from all over to establish their cotton plantations.

The community developed rapidly and an Indian agent wrote that "when civilization and refinement shall be well established, this will be a desirable part of the United States." Men were hired to lay out the streets with instructions to "let the plan of the town be as dashing as possible and

Anita Hoodless

All the beauty of a Huntsville springtime is captured in these lovely peonies.

the ground on which it shall stand as eligible as may be."

The fertile land had come to the attention of rich tobacco planters in Petersburg, Georgia. Practically *en masse*, they arrived, so many in fact that the town of Petersburg ceased to exist. The "Georgia Faction" began to dominate the political scene. In 1808, their leader, LeRoy Pope, bought John Hunt's land out from under him when Hunt failed to pay the registration fees to hold his land. Adding insult to injury, Pope renamed the town Twickenham, after the home of London poet Alexander Pope. In retrospect, it could have been America's tenuous relationship with England or Pope's manner that flew in the face of the townspeople, for less than two years later, the town was given a new and permanent name – Huntsville.

Hostilities with the Indians simmered until August 1813 when the Ft. Mims Massacre in Baldwin County sent shockwaves across the country. In October, word spread that the angry Creek Indians were within a day's march of Huntsville where they planned another massacre. Panicked residents dropped their work and ran toward Nashville and safety. But it had all been a hoax. General Andrew Jackson, a tall lanky Tennessean, had been summoned to put an end to the fear of Indian attacks. His militia stayed at the present-day corner of Holmes Avenue and Lincoln Street and another camp was set up at present-day Brahan Springs. Among his men was a crack shot Tennessean named David Crockett. The Creek Indian Wars ended,

---

Lily pads are islands of beauty to water creatures and insects.

Terri Shows

once and for all, with the March 1814 Battle of Horseshoe Bend. A celebration of peace was held at the fine mansion of LeRoy Pope where glasses were lifted in toasts long into the night. At that historic party were a number of future Alabama governors and, of course, a future U.S. President.

In 1817, the area known as the Mississippi Territory was divided when Mississippi attained statehood. The Alabama Territory followed two years later. The Constitutional Convention, held in Huntsville in July 1819, brought the best and brightest of the state to forge the constitution, which was considered quite progressive at the time. It was the first of many of Huntsville's shining moments. Several future governors and even a future vice-president, William Rufus King, served as delegates. Huntsville served as the provisional capital until the town of Cahaba could be readied for that honor. John Williams Walker, president of the convention and the first senator from Alabama, gave his closing address to the delegates on August 2:

"The subject on which we were called to deliberate was of the first importance. Our labors are now at an end. We have given to the State of Alabama, a constitution – not indeed perfect...yet it is emphatically Republican, and as such gives us a clear and indisputable title to admission into the great family of the Union...."

An Uncivil War

For the next forty years, Huntsville prospered and grew. King Cotton was the name of the game and farmers brought their bales to Cotton Row to be graded and sold. By the 1850s, the railroad rumbled into town and an enthusiastic spectator at the 1855 celebration proclaimed it "the greatest day in the history of Huntsville since John Hunt!"

But soon the rumblings of progress were overshadowed by the angry threat of war. Late into the night, prominent men met by the light of crackling fires to discuss the "whys," "why nots," and "how tos" of a civil war. The majority of Madison County residents had been opposed to secession, yet it was Huntsville resident Clement Claiborne Clay who bitterly announced Alabama's secession to the U.S. Senate on January 21, 1861. Clay's image would soon grace the face of the Confederate $1 bill. Slaves listened and watched in silence, waiting patiently for the day they would finally be free of the shackles that bound them to another human being.

Huntsville leaders were still arguing the issue of secession when another Huntsville native, Leroy Pope Walker, the new Secretary of War for the Confederacy, sent a telegraph to Charleston on April 10. He demanded the immediate evacuation of Union troops at Ft. Sumter. But Union Major Anderson refused, and the order to fire was given by Walker.

After thirty-four hours, the bombardment ended with the surrender of Union forces. The triumphant Confederate Secretary of War made a speech that day. Walker said "the flag which now flaunts the breeze here will float over the dome of the old capital at Washington before the first of May." He then said that he would take his pocket handkerchief and wipe up the blood shed as a result of the South's withdrawal from the Union. It marked the beginning of four horrible years of blood-soaked battle grounds, scorched earth, and utter devastation.

In the early morning hours of April 11, 1862, an army

Denise Raby

Through wavy glass windows of Alabama Constitution Village, visitors can look back in time to the exact spot where Alabama's first constitution was written.

---

of nearly 6,000 strong, under the command of Brigadier General Ormsby Mitchel of the Third Division, Army of the Ohio, entered Huntsville and captured the Memphis & Charleston Railroad Headquarters. A Union spy in the telegraph office intentionally failed to send the urgent message for help from the Confederate Army and the town of Huntsville was completely caught off guard.

"Truly our town is full of the enemy," Huntsville resident Mary Jane Chadick wrote in her diary. Those who had ridden the fence separating the union and the secesh, no longer wavered. Huntsville would remain occupied, off and on, for the remainder of the war. Unionist George Washington Lane defiantly flew his American flag over the porch of his home, fanning the flames of angry neighbors. Union troops burned the black church where the slave Bartley Harris preached. Future U.S. President James Garfield spent time in Huntsville while conducting the trial of Union Colonel Ivan Turchin, accused of atrocities against the residents of nearby Athens.

Fortunately for the people of Huntsville, they were spared the losses felt by the neighboring towns. Union officers enjoyed taking quarter in the large Greek Revival mansions, and even if they had time to resist the initial takeover, there were no men left to fight. They had already been consigned to battlefields and graves far away.

After four weary years, the war was finally over. The dead were buried and the living rolled up their sleeves to start over. Among those who returned were several former Union soldiers who had fallen in love with Huntsville's beautiful women!

A Time to Mend, a Time to Heal

The era of Reconstruction was a time of struggle. Freed slaves worked to find their place in society. Many people were bankrupted and impoverished. Some former slaves, having no skills, went to work for their former masters, this time as paid employees. They still had difficulties; they had no medical care and they now had to pay for room

Caroline Wang

Cotton, as far as the eye could see, was once the backbone of the Huntsville economy.

Patricia Hrivnak

The one-lane iron bridge at Ditto Landing was where Judge W. T. Lawler took his last breath. The life-and-death struggle, dubbed "The Crimson Murder," made headlines in 1916.

---

and board. But glory halleluiah! They were finally free.

In 1870, a freedmen's school was established. In 1872, the black church, which had been burned during the Civil War by Union soldiers, was rebuilt with money appropriated by President Ulysses S. Grant. It was named St. Bartley's Primitive Baptist Church, in honor of their beloved leader Bartley Harris. These were baby steps toward equality and integration which was still decades away, but it was finally a beginning.

Huntsville underwent another major transformation. Yankee money built cotton mills and each mill spawned entire communities, complete within themselves. The first, the Huntsville Cotton Mill, was built in 1881. It was the same year the Colored Normal School, predecessor of Alabama A&M University, was established with William Hooper Councill, a former slave, as its first president. The Huntsville city schools opened in 1875. Progress wasn't welcomed by everyone, however. In 1887, four electric street lights were installed around the square. "The light is abominable!" the local editor wrote with a demand that the city get rid of them.

In 1892, the City of Huntsville fell in love. Lily Flagg had big brown eyes and tanned skin and people came from all over to see Miss Lily. She also had two horns, four legs and an udder. The Jersey milk cow, owned by Samuel Moore, was about to break a world record for the production of cream. Parties were held in her honor and food made from her milk, cream, and cheese, was served to delighted guests. Miss Lily broke the previous record and won a blue ribbon at the Chicago World's Fair.

In 1898, the United States was again embroiled in war, but this time North and South fought under the same flag. The Spanish-American War, fought in Cuba, re-united a badly divided country. After the brief conflict, 15,000 war veterans came to Huntsville to recover from yellow fever because a government study had found that Huntsville's climate was the second most healthy in the U.S. Among those troops were the 9th and 10th Cavalry, the all black units known as the Buffalo Soldiers, under the command of "Black Jack" Pershing.

Dallas, Merrimack, Lincoln, West Huntsville, Lowe, and Abingdon were just a few of the sprawling cotton mills established in Huntsville. Thousands of people were employed to keep the looms humming, including young children. When the Child Labor Law went into effect in 1909, ordering that all children between the ages of twelve and sixteen attend school for eight weeks of the year, mill operators screamed that they would be forced to close. Labor unions were already threatening productivity and organizing strikes. Conditions for the workers were slowly beginning to improve, but at what price? Many lost their jobs and the mills struggled to keep their doors open.

A new cash crop was making the scene, however. The mild climate and limestone springs were the perfect environment for growing a delicate and tasty plant called watercress. Streams were dammed to flood fields and form shallow lakes and ponds to grow the watercress which was cultivated to produce up to five crops in good years. Huntsville became known as Watercress Capital of the World. Barrels of watercress were shipped from the Huntsville Depot alongside bales of bright white cotton.

In 1916 Huntsville made national headlines. The body of Judge Thomas Lawler was found weighted down in a slough near Ditto's Landing. The case was quickly dubbed the "Crimson Murder" and the man accused was his missing rival in the political race for Circuit Court Judge. Two prominent Huntsville men mysteriously committed suicide, leaving notes indicating a connection to the murder. David Overton was captured in Tennessee several weeks later and returned for trial. He was found guilty in a sensational trial and sentenced to die. Shortly after he was transferred to Birmingham to await his execution, he slipped out of jail in an arranged escape and died in a shootout with Birmingham police. Some whispered that the shootout had also been arranged. Huntsville truly was a small town: All four of the men involved in the murder were buried at Maple Hill Cemetery and the widows of Judge Lawler and David Overton continued to attend the same church.

Within a month of Overton's death, the United States entered World War I. Edward Chambers Betts was the first man from Huntsville to enlist. He would go on to become the Judge Advocate General in World War II, a personal friend of General Eisenhower, and the man to organize the Nuremburg War Trials. Betts died of a heart attack before the trials ended and he was buried in the Luxembourg American Cemetery, the last American interred there, and near the burial spot of General George Patton.

Robert Sallee

Northside square, Huntsville, late nineteenth century, when Huntsville was the largest cotton-producing area in the state. Wagons with bales of cotton would congregate around the courthouse, waiting for cotton brokers on the Westside square to evaluate their goods.

Ann Caudle

A child listens through an open window as the banjo player picks away, reminiscent of times gone by.

While there were more burials conducted in Huntsville's Maple Hill Cemetery in 1918 than in any other year, they were not casualties of war. The Spanish Flu claimed the lives of 393 people, 294 in October alone, in Madison County. The epidemic which spanned a frightening four months, was believed to have been brought here by a Philadelphia soldier visiting relatives in the area. Church services were called off, schools, soda fountains, and theaters were all closed. The war in Europe was over, but in America, more than ten times the number of war casualties now lay dead from "La Grippe," the Spanish Flu.

On Black Tuesday, October 24, 1929, the nation was plunged headlong into the Great Depression. It was certainly not the best time for the Russel Erskine Hotel, the new skyscraper named for Huntsville native and millionaire Studebaker president, to open the doors to the elegant new hotel in January 1930. Russel Erskine lived in South Bend, Indiana, but local financiers looked to him for monetary help to build the hotel in his hometown. Within a few years, Erksine had killed himself, plagued by personal losses and financial troubles at the Studebaker Company.

Once again the world was at war. Luther Isom, the first Huntsvillian to die in World War II, lost his life during the bombing of Pearl Harbor. A fence was erected around the Big Spring to ensure the safety of the water supply. Senator John Sparkman worked to gain approval for a Chemical War Service Plant and an Ordnance Plant to be located in Huntsville. Huntsville Arsenal and Redstone Arsenal employed thousands, and for the first time, many women folded their aprons and went to work to help win the war for the husbands, sons, and sweethearts who left town to fight. It was a time of significant change. Newspaper articles pleaded with black people to come to the factories, too. Segregation would have to wait for a more convenient time.

Neighbors grieved for the war dead, then went back to work. German prisoners of war were held at Huntsville Arsenal. A Huntsville soldier who had been in the horrific Normandy Invasion wrote home that he was so proud to see, in the heat of battle, empty ammo boxes with the words "Huntsville Arsenal" stamped on them. The nation rejoiced when the war ended, but it was a bittersweet victory. Now many jobs would be phased out and another time of adjustment loomed on the horizon.

When One Door Closes

On November 4, 1949, it was announced that the Ft. Bliss, Texas, Rocket Office would be relocated to Redstone Arsenal. A German "prisoner of peace" named Dr. Wernher von Braun would head up his team of scientists that would come to Huntsville, along with nine hundred civilians and soldiers. By April 1950, 344 family members had completed their move and in May, Dr. von Braun and his family applied for U.S. citizenship. Their original six month stay in America would last a lifetime.

The people of Huntsville were wary of the newcomers. The Germans had been our enemy and now they were our neighbor. But their leader, Dr. von Braun, extremely intelligent and charismatic, worked hard to gain acceptance for his co-workers, and was successful. Soon the ladies of Huntsville were trading recipes for cornbread and grits for

Linda Morton

Harrison Brothers Hardware Store is a popular attraction for visitors. When the last of the brothers passed away, the Historic Huntsville Foundation purchased it from heirs and continues to operate it as half-museum, half-store.

strudel and schnitzel. But even the transplanted Yankees couldn't justify drinking sweet iced tea all year around!

A building boom, the likes of which had never been seen in Huntsville before, took off like, well, a rocket. The city was filled with people from every corner of the world hired to help support the rocket testing program. Discussions about "algorithm" and "velocity" were accented with "y'alls" and "fixin' to." Ante-bellum mansions in Twickenham were divided into apartments and school sessions were held in shifts to accommodate the families that came with the scientists.

Space Capital of the Universe

On October 6, 1957, the Russian satellite Sputnik was launched, pre-empting the United States in space and sending local rocket scientists into a frenzy. Von Braun pleaded with Secretary of Defense Charles Wilson to give Huntsville the contract to build and launch the first American satellite. Instead, it was given to the Navy, and their Vanguard Rocket, along with the satellite, exploded on the launch pad two seconds after the December 6, 1957 liftoff. On January 31, 1958, the Army successfully launched the *Explorer 1* Satellite aboard the Jupiter C Rocket. Dr. von Braun officially announced the successful launch and the city of Huntsville exploded in celebration.

The Rocket City became the Space Capital of the Universe. Astronauts trained here, yet Huntsville would not relinquish her cotton roots firmly implanted in the rich red soil.

On May 18, 1963, President John F. Kennedy made a visit to the Deep South city of Huntsville. Perhaps it was no coincidence that only two days earlier, the City Council voted to remove the signs for separate drinking fountains at the courthouse. The President visited with Dr. von Braun and addressed ten thousand people on a podium where Governor George Wallace also sat. Although the two men were on opposite sides of the Civil Rights war, no mention was made in public.

A defining moment in the Civil Rights movement occurred on June 11, 1963, when George Wallace barred black students from entering the University of Alabama in Tuscaloosa. Earlier that day in Huntsville however, Robert Muckel, a white student from Nebraska, attended his first class at the all black Alabama A & M College. He had unintentionally already crossed the boundaries into the world of integration. Two days later, David McGlathery, a black graduate student, enrolled at the University of Alabama in Huntsville without incident.

That September, Sonnie Hereford IV entered Huntsville's Fifth Avenue Elementary and became the first black child to enroll in a white public school in the State of Alabama. The headline in the newspaper reported that "State Bars Negroes Elsewhere, Huntsville Quietly Integrates." No one in Huntsville was surprised. Signs of segregation had already been removed from Redstone Arsenal in 1952.

Rocket development flourished and Huntsville continued to grow. The January 1967 tragedy inside the *Apollo I* capsule that killed three promising young astronauts hurt the city deeply. Schools were named in honor of Gus Grissom, Edward White, and Roger Chaffee, as were later schools to honor the crews of the *Challenger* and *Columbia* after the tragic explosions which took their lives. We would never forget.

Huntsville celebrated another historic milestone when *Apollo 11* landed on the moon with the help of Huntsville's Saturn V Rocket. Sadness would come a few months later when Wernher von Braun announced he would move to Washington D.C. A day before his family left for their new home, it was announced that a $10 million civic center would be built and named in his honor. He left an enduring legacy, including the Alabama Space and Rocket Center, an interactive museum he envisioned would encourage young students to soar into the clouds. Dr. Wernher von Braun died in 1977, yet some of the original members of the "Paper Clip Scientists" still call Huntsville their home.

Tragedy in Paradise

The distinct four seasons make the Tennessee Valley a great place to live. Winters are fairly mild, and summers are not unbearably hot, but Mother Nature occasionally has a bad side. Over the last two hundred years, several tornadic events stand out, but in recent years, the two worst occurred in 1974 and 1989.

On April 3 and 4, 1974, an outbreak of tornadoes left seventeen people dead in Madison County. That particular tornado blitz hit thirteen states and lasted sixteen hours, leaving a total of 330 people dead and five thousand injured.

On November 15, 1989, the "Airport Road Tornado" became the worst on record. An F4 tornado with winds up to 260 miles per hour cut a half-mile swath up Airport Road at four-thirty in the afternoon—the beginning of rush hour. More than $100 million in damage was reported on that stretch alone. Sadly, twenty-one people were killed and 463 injured. In the reconstruction process, a brick memorial wall was built in front of Faith Presbyterian Church on Airport Road. Twenty-one bricks stand out in front of the others, one for each victim. A plaque was installed "in tribute to all who united for care and recovery."

Huntsville Reinvented

Today Huntsville is sometimes described as a cosmopolitan city dropped into the Old South establishment. Family pedigrees have been replaced with PhDs. It really is "rocket science!" Still, the Southern charm of Huntsville is appreciated by the many military men and women who are stationed here for awhile, move on, but come back to enjoy retirement in a town where they can donate their time and talent to make a difference. An impressive art museum overlooks Big Spring Park. The Historic Huntsville Depot Museum offers a glance back in time where captured Confederate soldiers were imprisoned on the third floor of the museum. Their thoughts, their names, their drawings, including an eerie peace dove, have been preserved as historic graffiti on the walls. Looking out through the wavy glass one can envision the trauma of Huntsville's capture in the Civil War, yet inside the silent walls hide the memories, and perhaps a ghost or two, of those who walked out onto the passenger platform to serve our country in world wars. Some would never return. Today the museum teaches children and adults about the history of railroads and the hardships of a Civil War soldier. Although no longer a passenger depot, the ground still rumbles as approaching trains pass by; their clackety-clack and screeching whistle complete the experience.

The U.S. Space and Rocket Center attracts visitors from all over the world to experience, touch, and learn about the wizardry of rockets. Dr. Wernher von Braun had hoped that a science-driven theme park would be every bit as successful

Caroline Wang

The magic of the space program is captured in this painting by artist Caroline Wang, and points to Huntsville's major industry.

as an amusement park and he used his influence to gather the exhibit items that serve as focal points. With the addition of Space Camp, it has the ability to touch every generation.

Alabama Constitution Village is a re-creation of the

buildings that were present at the very spot where our early leaders hammered out Alabama's constitution. Visitors learn about the everyday life of early residents, visiting the blacksmith shop, the post office, the surveyor's office, and the very place where the esteemed men met. One can almost hear the ghosts of Thomas Bibb and Gabriel Moore as they argue about who has the right to vote and watch the ghost of Clement Clay squirm during the discussion of how best to punish men for engaging in duels (he having already been in one).

The ante-bellum home of Maria Howard Weeden is the only once-private home now open for tours. She became a well-known portrait artist after the Civil War, renowned for her detailed drawings of former slaves, as well as the poetry she wrote about them.

The Huntsville Botanical Garden continues to grow by leaps and bounds, thanks to talented and creative volunteers. They are the retired engineers, teachers, homemakers, and nature lovers. A spectacular nature center/butterfly house has just been completed. Thousands come to see the ever-growing Galaxy of Lights during the Christmas holidays. Businesses and civic groups compete every fall to design the most outrageous scarecrows for the annual scarecrow trail. Visitors are encouraged to stand under the waterfall as it cascades in front of them or walk through the ribcage of a dinosaur in the Children's Garden, all the while enjoying exotic flowers and plants.

An interactive museum, SciQuest, is a place for children to learn and enjoy the fun that science has to offer. The exhibits appeal to a child's "gross-out factor" and keep the adults laughing for days. The EarlyWorks Children's Museum

The Steamboat Gothic House on Lowe Street, named because of the resemblance to a paddle-wheel steamboat, was moved from its original location, one of many Huntsville structures that have been protected by the Historic Huntsville Foundation.

Sherman Barnes

exhibits all phases of early life in Alabama and encourages children to dress up in pioneer clothing, participate in the Constitutional Convention, and learn about the Alabamians whose contributions helped change the world we live in.

The Burritt on the Mountain Museum is on a beautiful vantage point, popular for weddings and family reunions. Visitors play with live animals, watch men and women demonstrate crafts, and wander through restored cabins, a chapel, and of course, the home of the late Dr. Burritt. For those with an interest in the history of warfare, the Veterans' Museum is an excellent place to see actual uniforms, weapons, and tanks of America's wars. Alabama's only "40 et 8" boxcar, a gift from France, is on display at the museum, carefully tended to, as are all exhibits, with the help of the many retired veterans living in the area.

Huntsville has an astonishing number of talented individuals. The Huntsville Art League store showcases the work of local artisans, while those who enjoy singing and acting are encouraged to participate in the many performances sponsored by such organizations as Fantasy Playhouse, Renaissance Theatre, Theater Huntsville, IMP (Independent Musical Productions), and the Huntsville Community Chorus.

Other venues for showcasing their talents are the annual Maple Hill Cemetery Stroll, a fund-raiser to restore the old headstones at the historic cemetery. Locals dress in costumes of the era and portray the people buried at Maple Hill. Among the notables are five Alabama governors; David Todd, brother-in-law of Abraham Lincoln; and the many leaders and interesting individuals of the community.

Huntsville's big attractions include the annual Big Spring Jam, a weekend event in September to enjoy first class music of all genre, and the Panoply of the Arts, a celebration of art at the Big Spring Park, which is held every April. The Whistle Stop Festival and Rocket City Barbecue, held every May at the Historic Huntsville Depot, is KCBS (Kansas City Barbecue Society) sanctioned and attracts top notch competitors as well as entertainers.

The annual Cotton Row Run and the Rocket City Marathon attract upwards of a thousand serious marathon runners. Several historic organizations, such as the Civil War Roundtable, the Huntsville-Madison County Historical Society, and the Historic Huntsville Foundation provide venues to explore history with experts and amateurs alike. Several times every year, a few of the homes of Twickenham Historic District, Old Town Historic District, and Five Points Historic District are opened for visitors to learn about the people who made Huntsville what it is today. Even George Washington Lane's home is opened occasionally. Although his neighbors during the Civil War did not appreciate the American flag on his porch, every resident since then has flown a flag in his honor.

For those who like to wander through caves, a spelunker organization keeps like-minded individuals busy exploring the many area caves. For those who enjoy researching and reading, the Huntsville-Madison County Public Library is known far and wide for its impressive collection.

Through the years of struggle and strife, the Big Spring remains the sparkling jewel of downtown Huntsville. Surely John Hunt would be proud if he could see it today. Squealing children toss morsels to noisy ducks while the young and young-at-heart fall in love as they stroll along the banks that were once John Hunt's front yard. Indeed, Huntsville, Alabama is a flourishing town.

Chuck Long

Panoramic view of Huntsville from a walking path at the Burritt Museum on Monte Sano Mountain.

28

A woodland view from the Japanese Tea House.

Linda Morton

One of the most anticipated joys of childhood—selecting your own pumpkin for Halloween.

Malinda McCleary

Linda Morton

The pensive face of a little girl is captured in stone to grace a beautiful flower bed at the Huntsville Botanical Garden.

Debbie Sketo

The first Jewish citizens arrived in Huntsville in the 1840s; Temple B'Nai Sholom was dedicated only thirty-five days before the turn of the last century. It is the oldest synagogue in Alabama in continuous use.

Debbie Sketo

Billy Herrin

This lovely nineteenth century spiral staircase can be seen in Huntsville's First United Methodist Church.

Malinda McCleary

The North Alabama Railroad Museum in Chase, just north of downtown, features preserved railroad equipment, including three locomotives, and train excursions.

The 1860 headquarters for the Memphis & Charleston Railroad was captured by Union soldiers in April 1862. Confederate soldiers were kept as prisoners-of-war on the third floor until their transfer to Camp Chase. Their drawings and thoughts—Civil War graffiti— remain on the walls for visitors to see.

Judith Fields

Chuck Long

This painting shows the Huntsville rail yard in the late 1970s. Huntsville was a main point for both freight and passenger travel on the old Memphis to Charleston line.

Chuck Long

Burritt on the Mountain, A Living Museum, has been voted by Rand McNally as a top travel destination. Dr. Burritt built his house on the highest point overlooking Huntsville and left it to the City. Stories of his eccentricity abound.

Irises in bloom on a warm spring day brighten the façade of this old house.

Terri Shows

The woods around Huntsville are filled with wildlife. This charming raccoon has found a comfortable resting place inside the hollow of a tree.

Dorothy Montgomery

Harriett Dobbins

A lone fisherman has found a cool spot to drop his line in the water, and sit back and wait for a nibble.

Peggy Montano

The Japanese Tea House atop Monte Sano State Park is a reflection of the international feel embraced by Huntsville residents.

Lush green vegetation embraces the twisting Bankhead Parkway that leads up the backside of Monte Sano Mountain.

Leslie Lockhart

The altar of the Episcopal
Church of the Nativity, framed
by three lovely stained glass
windows, is the focal point
of this painting. One of the
oldest churches in Huntsville,
it has been home to many of
the 'old Huntsville families'
who trace their ancestral ties
to early church history.

Denise Schiber

Legend says that Union soldiers, ordered
to stable their horses inside the Episcopal
Church of the Nativity, refused after
reading the words over the doorway,
'Reverence my Sanctuary.'

Denise Schiber

Known as "The Marble Palace," this Greek Revival ante-bellum bank was designed by Huntsville architect George Steele. Although the bank's name has changed over the years, it is the longest continually used bank building in the state. It faces the Courthouse square, with the back wall overlooking the bluff of the Big Spring.

M. J. Montgomery

The old Councill High School, named for Dr. William Councill, an early president of Alabama A&M, was the traditional black school for many years prior to integration, and many prominent citizens of Huntsville today are alumni of this school.

Ben Patton

The bright white church and steeple of the First United Methodist Church in Huntsville has served the community for nearly 150 years.

Chuck Long

S. Renee Prasil

Almost every child in Huntsville grew up attending productions of Fantasy Playhouse, a theatre group that produces children's plays. Two of the most famous characters are Fantasy and Fantasy Jr., dressed as jesters, who introduce the plays and skillfully instruct the children in theatre etiquette.

Carole Forêt

The nationally accredited Huntsville Museum of Art fills its seven galleries with a variety of exhibitions throughout the year. In addition, the museum has an impressive 2500-piece permanent collection. The museum has been named as one of the state's Top 10 Travel Destinations.

First United Methodist Church, fondly referred to as the church with the purple doors, dates back to 1821. The original structure was accidentally burned by Federal troops during the Civil War. The cornerstone of the present sanctuary was placed in 1867.

Connie Watts

Many wonderful architectural features are found on the historic buildings of Huntsville.

Susan Clanton

Ed Starnes

The turn-of-the-century VanValkenburg house on the corner of Williams and Madison streets was built by a former Union soldier who liked Huntsville and returned after the war. Many old-timers fondly remember attending school dances held in the ballroom inside.

Dorothy Montgomery

Cattle are cooling off in this pastoral scene on Jones Farm in Jones Valley in southeast Huntsville.

DOROTHY MONTGOMERY

Ben Patton

Lowe's Chapel, an African American United Methodist Church, celebrated their 130th anniversary in 2006. Their original church, shown here, served the congregation for over one hundred years.

Snowball (Annabelle) Hydrangeas at the Huntsville Botanical Garden are lovely on the bush or captured on canvas.

Janie Byers

Leslie Lockhart

The Hays Nature Preserve Hiking Trail adjoins the Robert Trent Jones Golf Course at Hampton Cove southeast of Huntsville.

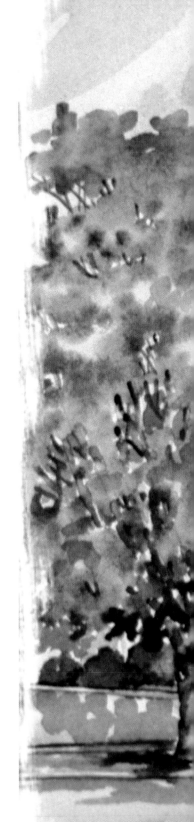

A quaint area of downtown Madison is quiet and peaceful on a Sunday morning.

Judith Fields

The Huntsville Depot Round House, a re-creation of the original located near the headquarters of the Memphis & Charleston Railroad, is now a popular place for parties.

Teresia Reid

Teresia Reid

The construction of St. Mary of the Visitation Catholic Church began in 1861. After a short interruption due to the Civil War, the building was finally completed. The church is made of native limestone cut from nearby Monte Sano Mountain.

Teresia Reid

Carole Forêt

Opposite page: The National Children's Advocacy Center campus is a state-of-the-art training center for individuals and organizations working to eradicate child abuse.

A very popular downtown Huntsville district on Washington Street, a remnant from the 1950s-1960s.

Carole Forêt

Goat Rock, near the fire tower at Monte Sano State Park, has been a point of sightings of feral goats since the 1950s. Perhaps descendants of escaped animals from Dr. Burritt's farm, as many as eight goats have been spotted at one time.

Katrina Weber

Judith Fields

A sleepy afternoon in the town of New Market.

Judith Fields

An old cabin on Green Mountain rests near a walking path, and is enjoyed by walkers on a fall day.

Jerry Brown

An old gnarled tree in the Huntsville Botanical Garden exudes personality, and for obvious reasons is known as the "squirrels' picnic table."

Spring rains once collected in these ruins to the delight of children who watched the tadpoles swim about. Decades ago, this old tavern on Monte Sano was gutted by fire, but was recently renovated to host upscale parties and celebrations.

Ed Starnes

Harriett Dobbins

The Great Pumpkin waits in the pumpkin patch, ready for a visit from an eager child.

Dunnavant's Department Store sold fashionable clothing for the entire family in the mid-twentieth century.

Lara Isbell

Chuck Long

Old country barns are distinguished by the overhang that held a winch to lift cotton bales to the upper floor.

JANIE C. BYERS

The Schiffman Building on east Courthouse Square was the birthplace of Tallulah Bankhead, she of the husky voice, honey-colored hair, and trademark "Dah-ling" greeting for all. The building is a prime example of early Romanesque architecture.

Janie Byers

Lee Harless

Looking west toward downtown, the Federal Courthouse, razed in 1954, is flanked by the steeples of the Episcopal Church of the Nativity on the left and the Methodist Church on the right.

FRED 00
SIMPSON

Fred Simpson

A rare snowy day is enjoyed by a solitary walker in front of Madison County's fourth courthouse. Built in the mid-1960s, its modern façade was chosen to reflect the desire of local leaders to look toward the future, in conjunction with Huntsville's Rocket City legacy.

This painting of one of the early rockets reminds the city of its space-age history—and future.

Carla Swinney

Huntsville was a sleepy cotton town before the rocket industry emerged, thus the descriptive phrase for Huntsville: "From Cotton to Rockets."

Linda Morton

Ed Starnes

The skyline of Huntsville, beyond the red bridge donated by Japan to the City of Huntsville, towers over our humble beginnings, the site of John Hunt's cabin.

Linda Ruhl

This one hundred-year-old dogwood was saved from destruction by caring citizens who paid to have it removed from an Old Madison Pike homestead. The tree was taken to the Huntsville Botanical Garden where it has thrived, thanks to the skill of garden horticulturist Harvey Cotten and his staff. The tree is twenty-three feet tall, forty-four feet in diameter, and had a root-ball weighing eighty-three thousand pounds.

The Huntsville Botanical Garden provides endless opportunities for artists to capture nature's beauty.

Harriett Dobbins

Carole Meredith

The Huntsville High School building in the early twentieth century is now home to the Huntsville City Board of Education, the central office for the Huntsville City School System.

Teresia Reid

The Gazebo at the Burritt Museum, overlooking the valley, is a popular site for weddings and other special events.

Carole Forêt

Five Points is one of three historic districts in Huntsville. The Star Market is practically a Huntsville landmark.

This attractive building is home to the Huntsville/Madison County Convention and Visitors Bureau, a vital source of information for visitors and hometown folks alike.

Carole Meredith

S. Renee Prasil

The Coffee Klatch (Kaffee Klatsch), a destination for morning coffee and evening entertainment, has become a downtown Huntsville institution.

L.Morton

The Saturn V Rocket is highlighted by another beautiful sunset—a manmade marvel surrounded by nature's beauty. The brightly lit landmark is a wondrous sight at night, as well as a source of local pride.

Linda Morton

Anita Hoodless

NASA, Redstone Arsenal, the Marshall Space Flight Center, and the Space & Rocket Center—and the establishment of hundreds of related companies—changed the face and the future of Huntsville.

Huntsville is on the tornado super highway. Cloud configurations like this one are carefully monitored by local weather forecasters.

Staten Tate

Terri Shows

A kneeling angel keeps quiet vigil over the grave of Mary Pittman Rice in Huntsville's Maple Hill Cemetery. This family is believed to be descendants of Pocahontas.

Historic Maple Hill Cemetery is the resting place of five Alabama governors, the first Secretary of War of the Confederacy, and many other historic figures. It is spectacular in every season, but especially in spring, when dogwoods are in bloom, and in the fall, when bright red and gold leaves peak.

Jerry Brown

Tim Prost

The late "Aunt Eunice" Merrill was the unofficial mayor of Huntsville. Politicians gathered at her breakfast restaurant to announce their candidacy, pour coffee, and rub elbows with many famous people who stopped in to eat ham biscuits at the Liars' Table.

The South is serious about barbecue and Huntsville is no exception. This pit barbecue establishment in rural Madison County is typical of the genre, and many proclaim it the best in the area.

David Kennamer

Mary Reynolds

This Southside view of the Huntsville Square shows Harrison Brothers Hardware (with two show windows) on the right.

Rachel Heeschen

In 2005 Huntsville celebrated its Bicentennial with a variety of events throughout the year.

Jerry Brown

On a bright spring morning, a young boy feeds the ducks at Big Spring Park.

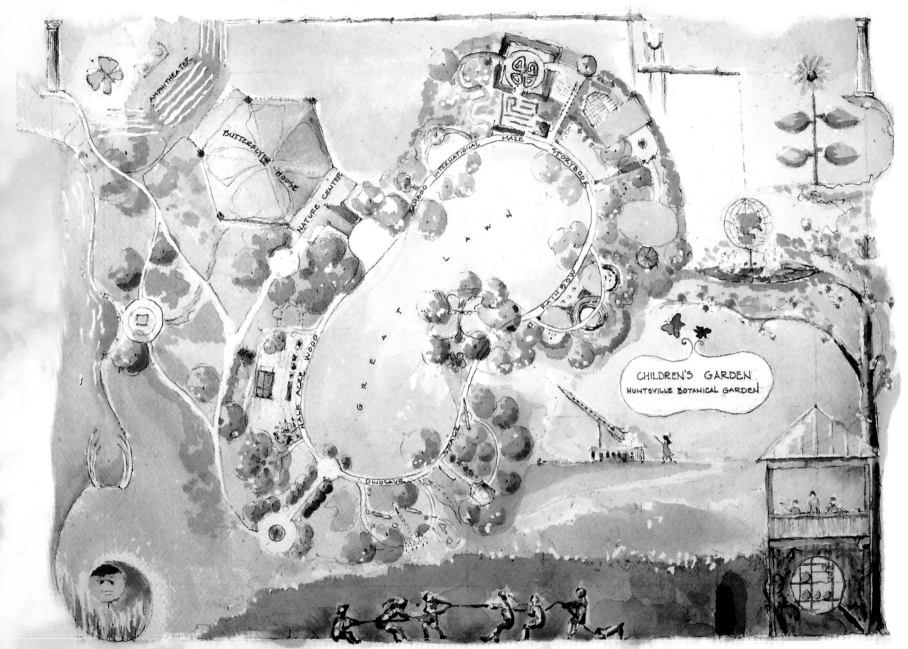

Carol Lambdin

The Children's Garden and The Open-Air Butterfly House and Nature Center at the Hunstville Botanical Garden provide fun activities and educational opportunities for all ages.

Linda Morton

The Galaxy of Lights, the ever-growing holiday event at the Huntsville Botanical Garden, is one of the Southeast's most popular attractions.

Daylilies are serious business at the Huntsville Botanical Garden. The Daylily Society is one of the Garden's much-appreciated volunteer support groups.

Helen Vaughn

Maggie Little

The Huntsville City Council voted to remove the 201-year-old oak tree from the middle of Adams Avenue in May 1956. An editorial in the Huntsville Times asked the Council to "go slow in cutting Historic Tree." For safety reasons, the tree had to go.

Heike Covell

Following a springtime shower, the sun has come out to create colorful reflections on the fast-moving Flint River. This lovely spot is located in Hays Nature Preserve.

Yeoman efforts have been made by the Burritt Museum to preserve homes of Huntsville's earliest settlers, such as the one shown here.

Jerry Brown

Jerry Brown

This woodland path is just one of the many beautiful areas of the Huntsville Botanical Garden.

M. J. Montgomery

This lovely setting invites visitors to sit and enjoy the Cottage Garden, one of the gardens that comprise the five-acre Central Corridor Garden at the Huntsville Botanical Garden.

The Church of Christ on Randolph Street was built in 1887 and has changed very little in appearance since then. The land it sits on was originally deeded to LeRoy Pope, the "Father of Huntsville."

M. J. Montgomery

Judith Fields

The leaves are just beginning to turn in this lovely river scene; the water spills over the fall, and autumn is on its way.

Jerry Brown

Big Spring International Park is the heart of Huntsville's past, present, and future.

The Summerhouse at the Huntsville Botanical Garden is surrounded by brilliant blooms of the Spring Festival of Flowers during April at the Garden.

Linda Steed

Pamela Watters

The gold dome at Parkway Place Mall represents the third shopping mall on this site. The first was destroyed by a tornado and the second demolished to make way for the modern construction we see today.

One of the many floral walkways at the Huntsville Botanical Garden.

Jerry Brown

The fabric of faith runs deep in Huntsville, reflected in it many icons of worship.

Danielle Damson

Huntsville Sketchbook Sponsors

U.S. Space and Rocket Center

For those fascinated with space, the U.S. Space & Rocket Center® (USSRC) is the best place on earth for exploration. Known as The Place for Space, the USSRC is home both to the largest space museum in the world and to the internationally-known SPACE CAMP® programs.

Visitors come both to learn more about current NASA programs and to see artifacts from the U.S. Space Program. An affiliate of the Smithsonian Institution, the USSRC has been privileged to host global corporate leaders, international space agency officials, top U.S. government officials, and children of U.S. presidents and celebrities. The museum, which is an agency of the State of Alabama, opened to the public in 1970 and has since entertained over 11.5 million people.

SPACE CAMP, which uses the mystery and wonder of space exploration to reinforce and to enhance learning in mathematics, science, and technology, has graduated almost 500,000 participants since opening in 1982. The SPACE CAMP curriculum is correlated to national math and science standards and draws during the academic year literally thousands of school groups that use the program as a supplement to classroom instruction. While the children who attend during the summer come for fun, many report back years later that the teamwork, leadership, and learning techniques they absorbed proved to be life-changing.

However, camp is not just for children. Corporate and government groups utilize SPACE CAMP as part of employee training programs. During June and July, hundreds of teachers attend SPACE ACADEMY® for Educators, a professional development program designed to instruct teachers in effective methods of presenting mathematics, science, and technology concepts in their classrooms. Camps for adults are held each fall.

While at camp, participants are taught in a unique environment called the ultimate classroom. The Mission Center Complex features shuttle simulators, a realistic mission control, and mock-ups of International Space Station modules where participants are immersed in the challenge of living and conducting experiments in space. Space history is taught in the museum complex that showcases the most complete chronology of launch vehicles in the country, including the Saturn V moon rocket that is designated as a National Historic Landmark. Other displays include the Apollo 16 capsule; a moon rock; a flown, manned, maneuvering unit; and astronaut training simulators. The nation's only full-scale, full-stack Space Shuttle exhibit, Pathfinder, is complemented by the shuttle exhibit, STS: The History of the Space Transportation System.

The USSRC's many interactive exhibits and public simulators make it particularly appealing to families. Rocket Park, located on the 80-acre USSRC complex, offers simulation experiences as well as space hardware described as "the finest rocket collection in the world" by retired astronaut and former U.S. Senator John Glenn. Rocket Park shows how Army rocketry initiated the Huntsville space program and spun off Marshall Space Flight Center.

The USSRC proudly serves as the Official Visitor Information Center for Marshall Space Flight Center, which remains on the forefront of space exploration. Also, the NASA Marshall Educator Resource Center, which serves educators in the six-state area of Alabama, Arkansas, Iowa, Louisiana, Tennessee, and Missouri, is located within the USSRC complex. The center is used extensively by teachers for resource gathering as well as workshops.

The combination of innovative technology and space artifacts makes the USSRC the nation's leading training ground for the next generation of explorers. Indeed, from committed space fans to those who are simply curious about the universe, the USSRC is The Place for Space. Come visit!

The museum, located at Exit 15 off I-565 in Huntsville, Alabama, is open from 9 a.m. to 5 p.m. daily except for Thanksgiving Day, Christmas Eve, Christmas Day, New Year's Eve, and New Year's Day. It is also home to one of the country's first dome IMAX® theaters.

Youth ranging in age from nine through high school seniors may attend camp. Children as young as seven years may participate with an adult in a weekend Parent/Child camp. Adult programs are also offered.

For admission prices or for more information about SPACE CAMP, visit www.spacecamp.com.

One Tranquility Base • Huntsville, Alabama • 35805-3399
1-800-63 SPACE • www.spacecamp.com

The University of Alabama in Huntsville

Imagine learning biology from a scientist whose experiments will fly aboard the space station. Imagine, as a student, designing an experiment, and carrying out that experiment in a zero gravity environment on a NASA airplane 36,000 feet above sea level over the Gulf of Mexico. Imagine learning from professors who are merging technology and the latest management techniques. Finally, imagine sitting in an engineering classroom and helping design a helicopter or a missile that may be used by the Army in the year 2020.

As a student, those opportunities would be too good to let pass by. These are real opportunities for students at The University of Alabama in Huntsville, one of the top research universities in the southeastern U.S.

UAH removes barriers between teaching and research. UAH professors take their research into the classroom, and UAH brings students into its world-class, cutting-edge research labs.

The university thrives on the synergy created by academia, government, and business that exists in North Alabama, which is enhanced by being located in Cummings Research Park, the second largest research park in America. The university complements the research and development needs of local industry as well as NASA's Marshall Space Flight Center and two major Army laboratories.

UAH's academic reputation has been recognized by Petersen's Competitive Colleges, and is the only public institution in Alabama to be rated a "very competitive" university by Barron's Profile of American Colleges and Universities. Incoming freshmen at UAH have an average ACT score of 25, highest among Alabama's public universities.

UAH has developed into a nationally recognized institution of higher education, valued for its research and prized for educational opportunities. UAH continues to excel in its scientific and engineering capabilities and also offers outstanding programs in liberal arts, administrative science, and nursing.

"The research of the university and its Ph.D. programs, with its concentration in engineering and science, has made us nationally and internationally visible," says UAH President Frank Franz. "Our companion programs in Administrative Science, Liberal Arts, and Nursing reach comparable levels of excellence within our region. We have focused upon building strengths that reflect the needs and interests of the broad-based community that we serve."

The university's core research strengths are found in propulsion, microgravity, materials, astrophysics, Earth science, optics, and information technology. UAH research activities produce close working relationships between faculty and students. The university gives students opportunities to apply their education in real-life job situations. More than seventy-five businesses, industries, and government agencies provide students with hands-on experience and often permanent employment.

The university provides activities outside the classroom such as intramural and intercollegiate sports, fraternities and sororities, choir and music ensembles, and theater productions.

While UAH offers a quality education, it also has impressive athletic programs, including a two-time national champion ice hockey team.

Scientific research and athleticism have come together to win honors for the university, such as in the five national award-winning entries submitted by UAH students who used their engineering and athletic skills to design, analyze, construct, and race a canoe made mostly of concrete. UAH students also have won national championships for the engineering, design, construction, and racing of a moon buggy. UAH students have repeatedly won awards in cooperative education, including the national cooperative education student of the year in 1998.

The university has more than 115 clubs and organizations, including the World Issues Society, Circle K, the Association for Campus Entertainment, and the Student Government Association. Greek life ranges from social activities to service projects for local and national charities. Six fraternities and five sororities are nationally recognized at UAH.

Athletics are a highly charged blend of competitiveness and the ideal of the student-athlete. The university is home to 13 NCAA men's and women's sports programs.

UAH is a shining star on Huntsville's horizon, expanding the universe of opportunities for both students and the high-technology community that surrounds it. As the world enters a new millennium, the men and women at UAH continue to look into the future and to help provide a vibrant vision for our area and our nation.

UAH
The University of
Alabama in Huntsville

Office of University Relations
Director, Joel C. Lonergan
256.824.6414

COLSA Corporation

COLSA's corporate culture reflects its roots in the Huntsville environment, as a dynamic and progressive, yet close knit organization. As a "Family of Professionals," the COLSA culture drives innovation, nurtures excellence, and empowers employees to provide state-of-the-art technology and solutions ensuring customer satisfaction.

A true American success story, COLSA is a highly successful engineering firm specializing in advanced hardware and software technologies, computer data center operations, and maintenance.

COLSA's success was recognized by its induction into the Alabama Engineering Hall of Fame. Celebrating its twenty-fifth anniversary in 2005, the company was founded in 1980 by retired Army veteran Francisco Collazo. Just eight years later, as a result of outstanding accomplishments under a variety of DoD contracts, COLSA was selected by the Small Business Administration as the "National Small Business Prime Contractor of the Year" — the first company to be independently nominated for the award by three government customers. Today, COLSA is a thriving multi-million-dollar business with more than nine hundred employees to support its many customers. The company's motto, 'A Family of Professionals,' has never been truer than it is today.

COLSA is headquartered in Huntsville, Alabama, with offices in Washington, D.C.; Shalimar, Florida; Orlando, Florida; Colorado Springs, Colorado; and San Diego, California. Its areas of core expertise include systems engineering, information technology, physical and information security, and programmatic support.

In centers where the DoD develops its weapon systems, COLSA designs and operates high performance computer (HPC) systems. Such precise engineering requires tremendous computer power—reliable giga-strength technology for which COLSA has earned a stellar reputation. The company's system integration expertise provides the Missile Defense Agency an Advanced Research Center environment in which to test system software, and to integrate hardware into the tests. At the DoD Missile and Space Intelligence Center in Huntsville, COLSA provides HPC and secure communications expertise. To support the Aviation and Missile Research, Development, and Engineering Center, COLSA integrated cluster computers to design and build one of the most powerful computers in the world.

When NASA conducts experiments on the International Space Station, it requires operational and scientific support and monitoring from the Huntsville Operations Support Center at the Marshall Space Flight Center (MSFC). COLSA is the contractor providing information technology support. COLSA personnel monitor the consoles and communicate with the astronauts in real time to help with any problems they may encounter. COLSA has provided NASA/MSFC with configuration management and data management support for more than seventeen years.

From its San Diego office, COLSA provides the U.S. Navy with tactical data link, command, control, and communication knowledge and shipboard communication expertise. COLSA's Shalimar, Florida, office provides Eglin Air Force Base with a variety of technical and management support services.

COLSA is also a turnkey solution provider of physical security solutions, including surveillance, intrusion detection, badging, and electronic access for commercial clients—such as Dynetics, BAE Systems, Boeing, Synovus Bank, and government agencies like the Missile Defense Agency.

Above all, COLSA strives to maintain its reputation for innovation and customer satisfaction. "It's not enough for us to be known as one of Huntsville's—and the defense industry's—leading high-technology companies," says Al Sullivan, president. "We're proud of the fact that COLSA is also known for its integrity as a provider of quality products and services to our customers, and as an active member in our hometown community."

COLSA Corporation
Corporate Headquarters
6726 Odyssey Drive
Huntsville, Alabama 35806
(256) 964-5600
www.colsa.com

Comcast

As the areas of technology and education are growing, Comcast Cable is growing with it. Comcast has grown from offering simple, analog cable to a state-of-the-art fiber optic system that offers the latest and most advanced in telecommunications products and services. Since purchasing the cable system in the City of Huntsville in 1986, Comcast has invested millions of dollars upgrading its cable system, offering the latest in technological advancements while remaining competitive in an ever-changing industry.

One of the leading communications, media, and entertainment companies in the world, Comcast boasts 60,000 employees serving more than 21 million customers. In Huntsville, Comcast serves more than 35,000 customers in the City of Huntsville and County of Madison. Comcast has come a long way from its start in 1963 in Tupelo, Mississippi, with only 1,200 customers and twelve cable channels.

"Our company credo states that we will be the company to look to first for the communications products and services that connect people to what's important in their lives," said Janine Morse, General Manager. "All of us at Comcast are working diligently to provide our customers with advanced telecommunications and entertainment services as well as providing quality customer service. We know what's important to our customers, and we want to be the first to deliver," continued Morse.

The past several years Comcast has delivered on its promises by offering new and advanced services such as Comcast Digital Cable, Comcast High-Speed Internet, and Digital Video Recorder (DVR). Two of the technological advancements that Comcast has deployed to its customers in the last year are Comcast Video On-Demand and High-Definition Television.

Comcast Video On-Demand is revolutionizing the way we watch television. Last year, Comcast surpassed one billion On-Demand program views from its customers. On-Demand views are IP streams of video content that are delivered to customers' television sets via Comcast's fiber network. Comcast On-Demand service offers a growing library of more than 3,800 programs available any time digital customers want to watch them – with the ability to fast forward, rewind, and pause selections. Nearly 95 percent of On-Demand programs are available at no additional charge. In 2005, Comcast added hundreds of hours of free On-Demand programs, including movies and TV shows.

High-Definition Television (HDTV) technology provides video and audio that is clearer, sharper, and more vibrant than ever, and Comcast is expanding its HDTV channels. Today, Comcast customers in Huntsville can watch local broadcast channels such as ABC, NBC, CBS, and Fox in HD. Other HD channels are ESPN, which offers more than 100 high-definition games a year, and IN DEMAND HD and IN DEMAND HD2 channels, offering an exceptional variety of sports, movies, travel, and nature programming. Premium channels such as HBO, MAX, Starz, and Showtime also offer high-definition programming.

Comcast is also very involved in the community and education. We have a strong commitment to improve the quality of life in our local communities where our customers and employees live and work. Last year, Comcast partnered with many great local community organizations such as the National Children's Advocacy Center, the Health Establishments at Local Schools (HEALS), Inc., and Alabama A&M, to name just a few.

Comcast's education initiatives add significantly to the learning experience for K-12 students. For every public school and library within its service areas, Comcast offers one free installation for cable and high-speed Internet. This connection enables schools to better prepare students for college and careers through the free use of cable and high-speed Internet. We also have developed a Leaders and Achievers Scholarship Program to help recognize high school seniors for their community service, academic achievement, positive attitude, and leadership skills.

"Comcast will be a strong corporate partner to the citizens of Huntsville and Madison County. We will continue to connect with people within our communities, and we will continue to make a difference through our education initiatives and community support," stated Morse. Comcast is making a difference—every day.

Comcast
2047 Max Luther Drive
Huntsville, Alabama 35810
256-859-7800

First Commercial Bank

The story of First Commercial Bank is a business success story, written in the language of hard work. To discover how strong, lasting relationships have been created and maintained, it is important to understand the principles and values First Commercial was created upon and has preserved as it has grown and prospered.

The story began in late 1983, when a group of local businessmen came together, intent upon opening a home-owned, independent bank to serve the Huntsville community. Citizens Independent Bancorp, a one-bank holding company, was incorporated in September 1983 for the purpose of opening a financial institution that put the needs of its customers above all else.

Financial partnerships formed with many small business owners as they founded their companies. These relationships flourished as the bankers became the business owner's trusted advisors. The success and growth of these companies has provided more jobs and improved the local economy.

In 1992, Synovus Financial Corporation, a multi-bank holding company located in Columbus, Georgia, acquired the bank. The bank's name has changed over the years to First Commercial Bank of Huntsville, yet the focus on business owner's needs has never wavered. Our personal relationships with our customers allow us to respond quickly. We are doing business with friends and neighbors, and our mutual interest in the community's growth guides our decisions.

While other large banks in our industry are merging and consolidating, we take a different approach. Our bank operates under a separate charter, we have a local CEO and a local board of directors - the responsiveness that is so essential to attracting and retaining customers still lies in the hands of our bank. Our local decision-making, personal service, and quick response are only half of the story. As a Synovus bank, we can also offer customers the full capacity of one of the nation's premier business banks. Synovus is a multi-billion dollar holding company that provides integrated financial services including banking, financial management, insurance, and mortgage.

This delivery model of **Community Banking, Powerfully Connected** allows small and medium-sized business owners to build strong relationships with local decision makers, while still gaining access to world class products and services. We have always believed our customers and team members come first. We treat others the way we want to be treated—and we believe that every day we must earn the right to serve you.

This is Our Customer Covenant:

We pledge to serve every customer with the highest level of sincerity, fairness, courtesy, respect, and gratitude, delivered with unparalleled responsiveness, expertise, efficiency, and accuracy. We are in business to create lasting relationships, and we will treat our customers like we want to be treated. We will offer the finest personal service and products delivered by caring team members who take 100 percent responsibility for meeting the needs of each customer.

First Commercial Bank

Strong Relationships. Powerful Solutions.

301 Washington Street • Huntsville, AL 35801
256-551-3300 • www.fcb-hsv.com

Alabama A&M University

Alabama A&M University (AAMU) has been around a long time. Since its founding in 1875, the north Alabama institution has become known throughout the world for its manner of achieving academic excellence without exclusivity. Having always opened its doors to all, the nearly 6,500-student university continues to offer students who need an academic boost an opportunity to excel beside internationally recognized student scholars. Indeed, for four consecutive years, the university placed students on coveted academic teams of USA Today. AAMU was also named one of the Top Fifty schools nationwide for African Americans by *Black Enterprise* magazine. From its modest beginnings as a land-grant institution in what is today downtown Huntsville, AAMU now boasts four (4) Ph.D. programs in the high-demand areas of food science, physics, plant and soil science, and reading/literacy.

Perhaps no better American success story exists than the Olympus in northeastern Huntsville fondly referred to as "The Hill." Known today as Alabama A&M University, it was founded in 1875 by William Hooper Councill, an ex-slave with the daring to dream big in a hostile American South. His legacy has ensured that the university is called "Alma Mater" by men and women throughout the world. The commitment to the education of all who enter its gates—where they are welcomed by the new Councill statue—has made AAMU an institution with one of the most diverse faculty bodies in the state of Alabama. Such diversity has spurred collaborations and numerous research opportunities.

Many companies also quickly tap into the school's expansive resources and benefit from quality and cost-effective research by a team of excellent campus scientists and researchers from the Schools of Agricultural and Environmental Sciences, Arts and Sciences, Business, Education, and Engineering and Technology.

The School of Engineering and Technology achieved much success under the deanship of Arthur J. Bond, who also founded the National Society of Black Engineers (NSBE) during his faculty days at Purdue University. In addition to programs in civil engineering and electrical, industrial, and mechanical engineering technology, the accredited engineering school recently has graduated its first class of scholars with full-fledged electrical and mechanical engineering degrees.

Moreover, AAMU faculty members are heavily involved in various aspects of research for numerous governmental agencies and subcontractors. In fact, the volume of research grants and contracts entered into by the university through its research faculty necessitated the development of the Alabama A&M University Research Institute (AAMURI). AAMURI adds professionalism to the business of pursuing, negotiating, and entering into contracts by university entities.

The most recent decade marked a period of significant renovations and construction on the hillside campus. The new 90,000-square-foot engineering school was completed, along with major renovations to the learning resources center and the campus's historic district. A lab facility for programs in food/animal sciences, plant and soil science, and forestry opened. A new agribition center for the School of Agricultural and Environmental Sciences and other local agricultural agencies is booked for rodeos, dog shows, horse shows, livestock events, and other activities through 2008.

This is an exciting time for the more than 130-year-old AAMU. Its scientists continue to work on projects as varied as the development of an allergen-free peanut, the study of volcanoes in the Caribbean, and research on plants that may prove effective in the treatment of diabetes. The list, like the need, is infinite, and people on "The Hill" are much too busy to boast for long. From the inexperienced entering freshmen, to the energetic and highly competent tenth president, Dr. Robert R. Jennings, the excitement on "The Hill" is contagious, and drives the university's progress into the future.

Postscript: Alabama A&M University boasts generations of outstanding alumni. Among them are William Cox, president, Cox Matthews & Associates, publishers of *Diverse Issues in Higher Education Magazine*, Fairfax, Virginia; Henry Gilford, CEO, Gilford Corporation, Beltsville, Maryland; John Stallworth, former Pittsburgh Steeler and inductee into the Pro Football Hall of Fame; and D.E. Wilcoxon, publisher, *Renaissance Observer*, Detroit, Michigan.

Alabama A&M University
4900 Meridian Street
Normal, AL 35762
www.aamu.edu

Crestwood Medical Center

Crestwood Medical Center has a lively and illustrious history, beginning in 1964, when it opened as a nursing home named for the subdivision where it was located. Since that time, visionary leadership has brought the hospital to its current incarnation as a part of Triad Hospitals, Inc., headquartered in Plano, Texas. An acute care 120-bed hospital located in southeast Huntsville, Crestwood has been in its current location off Airport Road in Southeast Huntsville since 1982, and soon will begin construction on a thirty-bed expansion that was recently approved by the Alabama Certificate of Need Review Board. This construction will add a third and fourth floor on the east addition, as well as a new four-floor structure to the north of the tower for administrative and support offices, allowing Crestwood to expand its licensed bed capacity to 150 total private beds.

With more than five hundred physicians on staff, representing more than fifty different specialties, Crestwood Medical Center is accredited by the Joint Commission on Accreditation of Hospital Organizations (JCAHO). A trademark of the hospital is the high degree of personalized care with which patients are treated. The staff is consistently ranked in the highest percentage of hospitals nationwide in patient satisfaction and leading-edge technology, blending high-tech medicine with personal care.

Crestwood's Centers of Excellence address patient needs in multiple areas and include:

Bariatric Center	*Maternity Center*
Outpatient Surgery	*Cardiology*
Special Procedures	*Center of Hope Cancer Care*
Clinical Laboratory	*Therapy Services & Sports Care*
Outpatient Diagnostic Services	*Women's Services*
Emergency Services	

One of the fastest growing and most successful Centers at Crestwood is Outpatient Surgery, where, thanks to modern technology and excellent training, most procedures, tests, and surgeries can be performed in the morning and have you back home by afternoon. Outpatient services afford patients the luxury of recovering comfortably in their own homes, and in familiar surroundings. This reflects Crestwood's commitment to making patients an integral part of their own health care, a commitment that is apparent in the range of services offered by the hospital as well as community education and prevention programs.

The Emergency Services department, with seven board-certified physicians and a full contingent of nurses and paramedics, treats everything from a broken bone to heart attacks and stroke. They provide fast, compassionate, and quality care to patients and family members. The number one disease in the United States is heart disease, and Crestwood Cardiac Care has expanded to meet the growing needs of the community. Emergency cardiac care is available twenty-four hours a day, seven days a week. In 2003, Crestwood joined a national registry that monitors patient outcomes for hospitals without onsite cardiac open-heart surgery. The Cardiac Care team at Crestwood exceeds the national average in moving the patient from the Emergency department to the Cath Lab to quickly and efficiently restore blood flow to the heart. The national average is approximately 107 minutes; the Crestwood team averages less than seventy minutes. Crestwood Medical Center also offers a variety of heart catheterization and endovascular procedures, including elective coronary intervention, arteriograms, balloon angioplasty, stent placement, catheterization, and pacemaker implants.

Crestwood Women's Center encourages women to take responsibility for their well being with regular check-ups, particularly mammograms and bone density tests. Breast Care at Crestwood Women's Center offers a multi-disciplinary approach to women's health concerns, ensuring that every aspect of the patient's need will be met. A team of professionals and a state-of-the-art facility promise quick results, and when necessary, referral to the area's finest surgeons and oncologists.

A community hospital known for its community spirit, Crestwood, its employees, and its volunteers support the Madison County area through sponsorships, donations, and volunteer time for organizations and events (approximately $1 million in 2005), including the American Heart Association, Huntsville Botanical Garden, Early Works, UAH College of Nursing, and United Way annual campaigns, to name a few. As a major contributor to the area's economic base by paying state and local taxes (approximately $1.7 million in 2005), and employing or affiliating with hundreds of health care professionals throughout the Tennessee Valley, Crestwood Medical Center plays a vital role in the area's economic health.

Crestwood has a proud history of service to the community and a tradition of excellence that will serve the citizens of Madison County well in the years to come.

Crestwood Medical Center
1 Hospital Drive
Huntsville, AL 35801
256-882-3100
www.crestwoodmedcenter.com

Madison County Commission

Barclay Burns '06

Nestled in the heart of the Tennessee Valley, surrounded by mountains, and blessed with rivers and streams, stands the space capital of America. The high-tech city of Huntsville, Alabama, county seat of Madison County, is known world-wide for its leadership in technology, space, and defense. It is, without question, one of the most progressive communities in the nation, and has come a long way from its frontier beginning.

Created in 1808 by the legislative body of the Mississippi territory, Madison County soon became home to the county seat after Georgia capitalist LeRoy Pope bought Hunt's Spring and surrounding acreage in what is now downtown Huntsville. The natural spring provided ample fresh water vital to the residents. Originally named Twickenham, the settlement's name was changed back to Huntsville by the territorial legislature. Pope's home was completed in 1814, and remains a prominent residence in the Twickenham Historic District today.

Cotton soon became king in the newly created Madison County. The area on the west side of the courthouse was known as "Cotton Row," thanks to the large number of cotton merchants, bankers, and lawyers located there. The first courthouse was completed in 1818 on the same site as the current Madison County Courthouse.

The Alabama Constitutional Convention was held in Huntsville in 1819. Alabama was admitted as the twenty-second state to the Union and Huntsville served as the temporary state capital.

The infrastructure continued to evolve in support of the cotton trade. Land and water routes from the downtown were completed to access the Tennessee River, a vital waterway for commerce. Further transportation improvements resulted in the Memphis & Charleston Railroad completion in 1855, making it easier and faster to transport goods to and from other areas of the growing country.

Beginning in April 1862, Huntsville was occupied by Union troops. In fact, throughout the Civil War, the city served as a communications center for Federal forces. Still visible is the graffiti left by Confederate soldiers held as prisoners of war on the second and third floors of the Historic Huntsville Depot.

The industrial revolution brought growth, with increasing numbers of textile mills operating in Huntsville after the war. The economy also diversified with the success of nurseries and fruit orchards. Huntsville had thriving watercress crops and soon became known as "The Watercress Capital of the World."

The turn of the twentieth century saw electric streetcars replacing horses and mules. The construction of major architectural landmarks, including the Times building and the Russell Erskine Hotel, highlighted the 1930s. During this era, the Tennessee Valley Authority was created, as well as other government agencies, providing much-needed jobs as the entire country began the slow recovery from the Great Depression.

The next decade saw the United States entering World War II. This became a crucial time for the Huntsville Arsenal as well as the Redstone Ordnance Plant as they played a vital role in the manufacture of artillery used in the war effort. The arsenal was threatened with closure in 1949, but was saved by the merger of the Huntsville and Redstone Arsenals and the opening of the Ordnance Guided Missile Center.

A significant event in the community's life came in early 1950 with the relocation of Dr. Wernher von Braun and his team of German rocket scientists from Fort Bliss, Texas, to Huntsville. The foothills of the Appalachian Mountains provided a striking resemblance to the dense forests of their German homeland and the team quickly adopted Huntsville as their new home.

The National Aeronautics and Space Administration (NASA) was created in 1960 and Marshall Space Flight Center opened at Redstone Arsenal. Dr. von Braun was installed as the first director, assembling a team of the best and brightest engineers to meet the tasks put before the agency.

The success of the team was unparalleled. From their work on the Redstone Rocket to the ultimate achievement of putting man on the moon with the Saturn V, this dedicated group of scientists and world-class engineers put Huntsville on the map as "The Rocket City."

In the decades since the Apollo missions, Huntsville and Madison County have continued to grow and prosper. Once the largest cotton-producing county in the state, Madison County is now one of the world's true high-tech Meccas. Often called "The Silicon Valley of the South," Huntsville/Madison County boasts a number of Fortune 500® companies with facilities located here. The quality of life is second to none, with some of the finest attractions and facilities in the nation available to our residents. A thriving economy with a broad base including manufacturing, government, corporate, tourism, and agriculture have served us well and poise our community for continued growth and prosperity throughout the twenty-first century.

MADISON COUNTY
c o m m i s s i o n

Madison County Commission
100 North Side Square
Huntsville, AL 35801

Fuqua &
Partners
Architects

BarclayBurns'06

Fuqua & Partners Architects (FPA) was founded in 1982 for the purpose of providing architectural and planning service for a wide variety of project types. In order to better serve its clients, FPA also provides Landscape Architecture and Interior Design so as to offer thoroughly integrated design solutions.

Fuqua & Partners has extensive experience in architectural, interior, and landscape design for projects involving new structures, additions, renovations, alteration/modifications, maintenance, and upgrades. The firm has completed over 3000 projects, providing services for buildings in Alabama, Tennessee, Mississippi, Georgia, Florida, Indiana, Oklahoma, South Carolina, Kentucky, and Louisiana. Many corporate/commercial businesses, government agencies, school systems, healthcare institutions, and churches have been served by the firm.

At Fuqua & Partners Architects we feel that Interior Design is an integral part of the architectural business. Not only should interior architecture complement the exterior aesthetic, but the interior should work hand in hand with the building envelope in order to provide the utmost sensory experience. Led by a Registered NCIDQ Interior Designer, FPA's Interior Design Department provides comprehensive interior design services including space planning, finishes, furnishings, modular systems, artwork packages, and applicable Code of Federal Regulations compliance for numerous projects.

FPA's Landscape Department is headed by a Registered Landscape Architect with more than thirty-plus years of experience in master planning, site and grading/drainage plans, landscape design, recreational parks, ball fields, parking studies, parking lot plans, and zoning changes.

FPA's architectural services are strengthened by an in-house former general contractor – grounded in sixteen years of construction – who directs our Quality Control and Construction Administration Department (CA). CA efforts are integrated at our firm in that the drawings are reviewed for construct-ability prior to issue and the specifications are written by our knowledgeable and experienced department staff. Submittals are checked for compliance with our contract documents and, if any deviations are noted, the contractor is required to revise and resubmit. Contractors' monthly pay applications are also submitted for review by the Architect and Construction Administrator and approval or adjustments are made prior to sending to owner.

The two main objectives of FPA's Construction Administration efforts are as follows:

1. To provide quick turnaround responses to contractor submittals and questions which helps foster a team approach and expedited schedules.

2. To act as the client's agent to assure that a quality facility is constructed per the contract documents, in budget and on schedule.

In addition to Fuqua & Partner's experience and technical skills, FPA is among the most respected firms in northern Alabama and surrounding states for its design ability and creativity, having received more than twenty significant design awards in the past decade. The best endorsement of FPA's professional performance is what their past and present clientele have to say about Fuqua & Partners. Such recognition is demonstrated by FPA's nomination for, and receipt of, the Huntsville/Madison County Chamber of Commerce Small Business of the Year Award in 1998 and the receipt of the 2004 AGC (Associated General Contractors of America) "Architect of the Year Award."

LEARNING BY DESIGN - A School Leader's Guide to Architectural Services has chosen several Fuqua & Partners projects to feature, including Russellville City Schools Fine Arts Center, Madison County High School of Madison County Schools, Bob Jones High School, and Rainbow Elementary School of Madison City Schools. Rainbow was also featured at the National School Boards Association meeting in San Francisco. FPA's library addition to University of Alabama in Huntsville, was showcased in *College Planning & Management* as well as the *Education Design Showcase Annual Awards Edition*. For the past several years, *Business Alabama Monthly* has ranked Fuqua & Partners as one of Alabama's Top-10 Design Firms. These recognitions reflect FPA's ability to provide the highest quality of professional design services.

Understanding and responding to the owner's needs and schedules have become a hallmark at FPA. Responding to the business realities of our clients has made our design solutions on target, creative, and efficient, while providing a better result for our clients. Fuqua & Partners' commitment to client satisfaction and professional integrity has molded the firm into an accomplished team with an extensive list of satisfied clients in the public and private educational sectors.

Fuqua & Partners Architects
112 Washington Street
Huntsville, AL 35801

The Artists

Danielle Damson
danielle@damson.com
Page 92

Billy Herrin
1698 E. Stonehurst Dr.
Huntsville, AL 35801
256.881.0654
wherrin@comcast.net
Page 31

Sherman Barnes
28532 Nora St.
Madison, AL
256.771.1266
sbarnes@knology.net
Page 25

Harriet Dobbins
114 Compass Point Dr.
Madison, AL 35758
256-325-4595
everythingmatters@earthlink.net
Pages 37, 60, 69

Dee Burt Holmes
1725 Drake Ave.
Huntsville, AL 35802
256.883.7122
wmholmes@mindspring.com
Pages 8, 11

Jerry Brown
2809 Barcody Rd.
Huntsville, AL 25802
256.883.5217
jerrybrown@knology.net
Pages 59, 77, 81, 86, 90, 92

Judith Fields
102 Memory Lane
Harvest, AL 35749
256.830.1780
www.judithfields.com
Pages 32, 52, 57, 58, 89

Anita Hoodless
1400 Appalachee Dr.
Huntsville, AL 35801
256.881.4565
Rhoodless590@cs.com
Pages 1, 10, 75

Ann Caudle
4411 Choctaw Circle
Huntsville, AL 35801
256.539.2194
anncaudle@comcast.net
Page 20

Carole Forêt
206 W. Market St.
Athens, AL 35611
256.232.2521
www.caroleforet.com
carole@caroleforet.com
Pages 45, 54, 55, 72

Patricia Hrivnak
710 Larry Dr.
Madison, AL 35758
256.772.7935
hrivnja@hiwaay.net
Page 17

Susan Clanton
901 Cleermont Dr.
Huntsville, AL 35801
256.533.0092
clanton25@comcast.net
Page 46

Lee Harless
1201 Locust Ave.
Huntsville, AL 35801
256.536.3659
Page 64

David Kennamer
P.O. Box 128
Guntersville, AL 35976
256.582.2216
kennd@charter.net
Page 78

Heike Covell
11012 Willingham Dr.
Huntsville, AL 35803
256.880.9661
stuttgart80@knology.net
Page 85

Rachel C. Heeschen
2200 Covemont Dr.
Huntsville, AL 35801
256.534.2854
rheeschen@bellsouth.net
Page 80

Carol Blair Lambdin, ASLA
Landscape Architect
Harvest, AL 35749
Page 82

Leslie Lockhart
4904 Preakness Cir.
Brownsboro, AL 35741
256.536.5110
leslie@leslielockhart.com
Pages 39, 51

Linda Morton
282 Knox Creek Trail
Madison, AL 35757
256.721.1601
joe.morton@knology.net
www.artistcolony.net
Pages 22, 28, 29, 66, 74, 83

Linda Ruhl
28044 Kim Dr.
Harvest, AL 35749
256.232.9791
www.lindasartworld.com
Page 68

Malinda McCleary
12109 North Gate
Huntsville, AL 35810
256.852.6189
marty@huntfast.com
Pages 29, 32

Ben L. Patton
185 Turner Circle
Harvest, AL 35749
256.837.1319
Pages 42, 49

Robert Sallee
Huntsville, AL 35801
256.883.7996
rsallee@bellsouth.net
Page 19

Carol B. Meredith
245 Jackson Trace Rd.
Titus, AL 36080
334.567.7056
bdaleart@aol.com
Page 70, 72

S. Renee Prasil
2740 Deford Mill Rd.
Hampton Cove, AL 35763
256.533.7329
smartartsR@aol.com
www.sreneeprasil.com
Pages 44, 73

Denise Schiber
134 Oak Brook Cir.
Madison, AL 35758
256.603.8113
www.artworkbydenise.com
Pages 40, 41

Peggy Montano
www.artistcolony.net/
    peggymontano
256.527.2673
pjmontano@aol.com
Page 38

Timothy J. Prost
timprost@us.army.mil
Page 78

Terri Shows
9916 Todd Mill Rd.
Huntsville, AL 35803
256.882.1427
terrishows@comcast.net
www.B17.com
Pages 12, 35, 77

Dorothy Montgomery
3128 Heather Hill Dr.
Huntsville, AL 35802
256.881.9527
jackmont1@comcast.net
Pages 36, 48

Denise Raby
1603 Greenwyche
Huntsville, AL 35801
256.533.0197
gunice57@aol.com
Page 14

Fred B. Simpson
7111 Heathrow Dr.
Huntsville, AL 35801
256.881.7459
fpsimpson@comcast.net
Page 65

M.J. (Martha) Montgomery
Huntsville, AL 35802
256.509.5163
mjmskyjack@aol.com
Pages 42, 87, 88

Teresia Reid
207 Wingate Ave. S.W.
Huntsville, AL 35801
256.881.2638
hreid2@bellsouth.net
Pages 52, 53, 71

Debbie Sketo
Debbies.art@comcast.net
Page 30

Ed Starnes
3505 Carroll Cir. S.E.
256.539.9093
Pages 5, 47, 59, 67

Connie Watts
428 Forest Hills Dr.
Childersburg, AL 35044
Page 46

Chuck Long
2803 Lafayette Rd.
Huntsville, AL 35801
256.534.9848
mlong94291@aol.com
Pages 27, 33, 34, 43, 62

Linda Steed
2104 Woodcliff Rd. S.E.
Huntsville, AL 35801
256.533.1016
lsteed@comcast.net
Page 91

Katrina Weber
3604 Mae Dr.
Huntsville, AL 35801
256.536.1397
chuckkat@pobox.com
Page 56

Artist not pictured

Pamela Watters
pam147@aol.com
Page 91

Carla Swinney
970 Tracey Ln. S.W.
Decatur, AL 35601
256.350.7741
cswinney970@charter.net
www.carlaswinney.com
Page 66

Janie Byers
byersjanie@aol.com
Pages 50, 63

**Photography provided by
S & S Photography**

Steve and Sandra Gray have been partners as S & S Photography since 1978. They are constantly striving to step outside their box, to keep their outlook on their business fresh, and their attitudes optimistic. Please feel free to call with any questions you may have.

Staten Tate
ST8NT8@knology.net
Page 76

Lara Isbell
1005 Clinton Ave.
Huntsville, AL 35801
256-457-3819
www.laraisbell.com
Page 61

S & S Photography
2365 Whitesburg Dr.
Huntsville, AL., 35801
256-533-0088

Helen J. Vaughn
703 Oak Park Dr.
Huntsville, AL 35801
256.534.4202
vaughmart@bellsouth.net
Page 83

Maggie Little
mlittleart@knology.net
Page 84

Caroline Wang
www.cwanggallery.com
Pages 15, 24

Mary Reynolds
romarrey@comcast.net
Page 79